Beds

A theatre piece in two acts

by

Anne Le Marquand Hartigan

CHISWICK BOOKS

LONDON

www.chiswickbooks.com

First published in 2016 by Chiswick Books
2 Prebend Gardens, Chiswick, London W4 1TW
email: info@chiswickbooks.com
website: www.chiswickbooks.com

Beds copyright © Anne Le Marquand Hartigan 1982
Anne Le Marquand Hartigan is hereby identified as author of this play in accordance with section 77 of the Copyright, Designs and Patents Act 1988. The author has asserted her moral rights.

All rights whatsoever in this play are strictly reserved and application for performance etc. should be made before commencement of rehearsal to email: rights@annehartigan.com. No performance may be given unless a licence has been obtained, and no alterations may be made in the title or the text of the play without the author's prior written consent.

This book is sold subject to the condition that it shall not by way of trade or otherwise be circulated without the publisher's consent in any form of binding or cover or circulated electronically other than that in which it is published and without a similar condition including this condition being imposed on any subsequent purchaser.

British Library Cataloguing in Publication Data. A catalogue record for this book is available from the British Library.

This is a work of fiction. Names, characters, places and incidents either are products of the author's imagination or are used fictitiously. Any resemblance to actual events or locales or persons, living or dead, is entirely coincidental.

ISBN: 978-1-910721-05-6

Cover image from a painting by Anne Le Marquand Hartigan.

Also by the author

Plays

I Do Like to be Beside the Seaside, *Chiswick Books, 2016*
Jersey Lilies, *Chiswick Books, 2016*
La Corbière, *Chiswick Books, 2016*
Three Short Plays, *Chiswick Books, 2016*
The Secret Game, *Chiswick Books, 2014*

Poetry

Unsweet Dreams, *Salmon Poetry, 2011*
To Keep The Light Burning, *Salmon Poetry, 2008*
Nourishment, *Salmon Poetry, 2005*
Immortal Sins, *Salmon Poetry, 1993*
Now is a Moveable Feast, *Salmon Poetry, 1991*
Return Single, *Beaver Row Press, 1986*
Long Tongue, *Beaver Row Press, 1982*

Prose

Clearing the Space, *Salmon Poetry, 1996*

To Robert Gordon, for our adventure together.

Beds was first produced by Moveable Feast Theatre Company as part of the Dublin Theatre Festival, October 1982 with the following team:

Cast	Daire Brehan
	Sean Campion
	Sarah Carroll
	Una Clancy
	Michael Cosgrove
	Al McKenna
	Paidraig Murray
Director	Robert Gordon
Composer	Eibhlis Farrell
Production Manager	Rosemary Valentine
Costume	Jacklyn Young
Lighting	Hugh Arnold
Stage Manager	Sean Campion
Percussion	Hugh Le Marquand
Graphic design	Jeremy Leland

With grateful thanks to the following artists who were involved in the workshop development of the script:

Actors	Bríd Brennan
	Robert Byrne
	Guy Carlton
	Liam Halligan
	Bairbre Ní Chaoimh
	Ann O'Driscoll
	Donal O'Kelly
	Joan Sheehy
Writers	Maeve Kelly
	Willy French
Musician	John Crowe

Characters

Pre-theatre piece

Sales Talk

ALL

VOICE ONE

VOICE TWO

Act One

Life-cycle mime

FEMALE A

MALE A

FEMALE B

MALE B

FEMALE C

MALE C

Foetuses

FOETUS ONE

FOETUS TWO

FOETUS THREE

TWO BLOBS

ANNE LE MARQUAND HARTIGAN

Ritual bedmaking

ALL

Boxing match

BRIDE

GROOM

BROTHER OF THE GROOM

MOTHER OF THE BRIDE

REFEREE

AGONY AUNTIE

ROUND ANNOUNCER *Played by a woman*

CROWD

Ritual bedmaking

ALL

Domestic violence

HUSBAND

WIFE

LISTENER

BOY

GIRL

Interval

USHERETTE

SEX SYMBOLS

Act Two

Loving couples

SEXY WOMAN

SEXY MAN

LOVING WOMAN

LOVING MAN

UPTIGHT WOMAN

UPTIGHT MAN

Ritual bedmaking

ALL

Three women alone

WOMAN ONE

WOMAN TWO

WOMAN THREE

Abortion

HUSBAND

WIFE

GIRL *Their daughter*

PRIEST

The Sacred Heart

GIRL

THE SACRED HEART

The three rooms of death

WOMAN

OLD MAN

YOUNG WOMAN

Marriage/Funeral

PRIEST *Played by a woman*

BRIDE

GROOM

GUESTS

Note

The titles of the actions or scenes of the play are for descriptive purposes only and were not used in the original programme, the actions flowing one into the other without a break. The play however, moves in a life-cycle from pre-birth to death of various kinds.

The song, 'In bed we laugh, in bed we cry,' is sung at intervals throughout the production to music composed by Eibhlis Farrell. This theme tune is adapted to different modes and moods as the scenes dictate. In the first production it was sung and danced to a Charleston, then honky tonk etc.

Ritual bedmaking occurs at different points during the production accompanied by music and theme song as the beds are moved to different positions to create mood changes. In the original production the audience also moved to cope with the challenges of the venue. Cream coloured sheets were used which were ritually folded and unfolded and smoothed down. Two actors standing, one either side of the bed, billowed the sheet upwards, then moved together slowly to fold it.

Pre-theatre piece

Performed in the foyer or theatre as audience arrives, to be adapted according to the venue. Utilises two rooms or spaces.

Room one contains three double beds. The audience wander through and around the cast as they perform 'Sales Talk.' At the same time, others in the cast speak factually about sleep.

Room two: The Bed of Dreams. All white and silent, a pure white double bed in the centre with white netting draped around it from a centre point above the bed. Peace, light dim, soft, kind. Sounds of gentle breathing. Whisperings of dreams. Audience enters, one by one if possible, and are invited to lie and dream on the bed, accompanied by dream music. Very peaceful voices and music interweave. This room remains for audience to re-visit at the interval.

Sales talk

ALL

Lines to be divided amongst cast.

Choose Silent Night. The one top people are settling on.

Choose this super de luxury, pride of our tribe. A bed sculpted by our crafts-persons, cushioned and cosseted with many and multiple layers of a new fabric unique to ourselves. This fabric, developed in our laboratories, gives a comfort as yet to be experienced by humankind. After three years of intensive testing it has been pronounced completely flea-proof. Any bed bug or creepy crawly who places foot or feeler on or near this miracle material drops dead. You will spend nights, nay, a lifetime without minor irritations. This is a bed of dreams.

The up-to-the-minute designs by our team of artists in fabric, have produced the finest quality jacquard that elegantly complements the tastefully quilted panels ornamenting the sides. This is a bed you will treasure for a lifetime.

Or

Choose Posturemedic. The bed for those with
back trouble.

Posturemedic with posture springing that
gives support where you need it most. Because
posturemedic is made in one continuous unit...

All the coils work together to spread the weight.

So neither partner rolls into the centre of the bed.

In addition, this greater support makes movement
easier. Designed with our senior citizens in mind.

A person changes position between thirty five
and sixty times a night. Posture-medic springing
follows every change in the shape of the body.
So no excessive pressure is concentrated on the
hips... every part of the body enjoys... comfort
and rest.

Please note, the design of our tasteful ticking
used, but not, of course, the superb quality, may
be changed without notice during the life of this
salesman, the life of this catalogue.

Helen of Troy: a bed fit for a queen and her
king. Delicate edge-to-edge quilting is a special
feature of this magnificent bed. We use attractive

coverings on the finest quality ticking over layers of pure cotton felt.

Pause.

Grown on our cotton fields back home.

Pause.

We have lavished thick folds of upholstery on the mattress to a depth of...

Pause.

Ten inches.

So your nights will be majestic. Your sleep the sleep of monarchs. No princess, we guarantee, could ever feel a pea through the quilted bliss of this bed. The spring-edge divan sports the same supporting and restful edge-to-edge spring unit for greater resilience and longer life. Sleep longer with Helen of Troy. For deep and healthy sleep, it's money well spent. You'll never regret the hours you've slept on a Helen. Ten years' guarantee.

From the House of Firmilux.

You need a firm bed? Then the original Ballymount is for you.

You are short of storage space? This new creation

has only just arrived at our bed centre, was
used in experiments at this year's Congress of
Insomniacs. This bed received a major award in
a 48-hour sleep-in, in the economy and comfort
class. So O Sweetest is proud to introduce to its
customers this bed, tailored with you in mind.
Covered in deeply dimpled damask with layers of
cotton and other natural fibre for cushioning the
Ballymount solves your problems of sleep and
storage. The base unit incorporates commodious
deep drawers, useful for the storage of blankets,
bed linen or children. There is a small drawer
near the bedhead for books, pencils, prayer
wheels, hair pieces, false teeth, contraceptives
and cough drops. Ballymount, the economy bed
in the O Sweetest range, brings new order to your
life.

VOICE ONE

In a pseudo-poetic voice.

Come sleep. Oh sleep, the certain host of peace.[1]

VOICE TWO

Speaks deadpan, factual.

What is sleep? It is a recurrent healthy state.

---

[1] Sir Philip Sidney, Sonnet 39, Astrophil and Stella.

VOICE ONE
>The baiting place of wit, the balm of woe.[2]

VOICE TWO
>It is the state of inertia and unresponsiveness.

VOICE ONE
>The poor man's wealth, the prisoner's release.[3]

VOICE TWO
>You do not respond overtly, having dozed off during the sermon.

VOICE ONE
>The indifferent judge between the high and low.
>
>Tired nature's sweet restorer, balmy sleep.[4]

VOICE ONE
>What happens when we fall asleep? The eyelids close and the pupils become very wide.

VOICE TWO
>He, like the world, his ready visit pays
>
>Where fortune smiles; the wretched he forsakes.[5]

VOICE ONE
>The secretion of saliva, of digestive juices and

---

[2] ibid.
[3] ibid.
[4] ibid.
[5] Edward Young, The Complaint, Night Thoughts.

urine falls sharply. The total flow of air breath is diminished. The heart slows.

VOICE TWO

Care charming sleep, thou easer of all woes.
Brother to Death...[6]

VOICE ONE

The electrical brainwaves change in character, reflecting a deterioration in the efficiency with which the brain can deal with the world around, consciousness is lost.[7]

VOICE TWO

Care-charmer sleep, son of the sable night.

Brother to Death, in silent darkness born.[8]

VOICE ONE

Birds certainly sleep and many do while standing on one leg...[9]

VOICE TWO

Relieve my languish and restore the light,

With dark forgetting of my care return.[10]

VOICE ONE

Cows, for example, sleep with their eyes open.

---

6   John Fletcher, The Tragedy of Valentinian.
7   Ian Oswald, Sleep.
8   Samuel Daniel, Sonnet 45 to Delia.
9   Ian Oswald, Sleep.
10 Samuel Daniel, Sonnet 45 to Delia.

and go on chewing the cud. We do not usually keep our eyes open, but we do keep our ears open.[11]

VOICE TWO

And let the day be time enough to mourn

The shipwreck of my ill-adventured youth.[12]

VOICE ONE

Dolphins have attracted a lot of research in recent years and appear to sleep for a couple of hours with first one eye and then the other open.[13]

VOICE TWO

Let waking eyes suffice to veil their scorn,

Without the torment of the night's untruth. [14]

ALL

Lead audience into theatre carrying the beds to the stage. Sing.

In bed we laugh, in bed we cry,

And born in bed, in bed we die.

The near approach a bed may show

Of human bliss and human woe. [15]

---

11 Ian Oswald, Sleep.
12 Samuel Daniel, Sonnet 45 to Delia.
13 Ian Oswald, Sleep.
14 Samuel Daniel, Sonnet 45 to Delia.
15 Isaac de Bernserade, translated by Samuel Johnson.

Act One

Life-cycle mime

Mime with honky-tonk piano music.
Three double beds in a row, left to right: Bed One, Bed Two and Bed Three.

> *MALE A and FEMALE A enter upstage centre, hold hands, move as puppets in time to the music Charlie Chaplin style. Walk downstage either side of centre Bed Two. Get into bed. Lie stiffly side by side. Mime copulation strictly in time to the music.*
>
> *Get out of bed, one pees, the other prays.*
> *Return to bed. Sleep.*
> *Wake.*
> *Mime rising, dressing, washing, eating, walking, crapping, peeing, sitting, saying goodbye, going to work, returning etc. Return to bed. Lie stiffly.*
> *Copulate.*
> *Lie stiffly.*
> *Sleep.*

FEMALE A gives birth as MALE A sleeps at her side. MALE B emerges from between FEMALE A's legs as a baby.

MALE B gives baby cry.

FEMALE A cradles baby accompanied by lullaby music.

Couple A express joy. One pees while the other prays.

MALE B sleeps.

Couple A return to bed and sleep. Now copied by MALE B, wake. Mime rising, dressing, washing, eating, walking, crapping, peeing, sitting, saying goodbye, going to work, returning etc.

All return to Bed Two.

Couple A remove the baby, MALE B, to Bed One.

MALE B objects

Couple A copulate

MALE B makes childish cries

Couple A, one pees, one prays.

MALE B sleeps.

Couple A sleep. Wake.

FEMALE A gives birth as MALE A sleeps at her side. FEMALE C emerges from between

FEMALE A's legs as a baby.

FEMALE C gives baby cry.

FEMALE A cradles FEMALE C accompanied by lullaby music.

Couple A express joy. One pees while the other prays.

FEMALE C sleeps.

Couple A return to bed and sleep.

Couple A wake, copied by MALE B and FEMALE C growing up during the following mime: rising, dressing, washing, eating, walking, crapping, peeing, sitting, saying goodbye, going to work, returning etc.

MALE B ends up in Bed One, FEMALE C ends up in Bed Three.

Enter FEMALE B and MALE C. Meet their partners. Love at first sight. All couples go to bed.

All lie stiffly in bed.

Copulate strictly in time with the music.

One of each couple pees while the other prays. Sleep.

Lie stiffly.

Snore.

Wake.

Mime rising, dressing, washing, eating, walking, crapping, peeing, sitting, saying goodbye, going to work, returning etc. MALE A becomes sick during this action unnoticed by the rest who continue on with the everyday mime. MALE A dies, head over the end of the bed towards the audience. He is noticed.

OTHERS

Small scream.

No music for four beats. Life goes on, the deceased is ritually but speedily shoved under the bed.

FEMALE A is now left alone. She moves into Bed One and COUPLE B move into Bed Two.

All lie stiffly.

Copulate, women on top this time, apart from FEMALE A who is becoming old.

Pee and pray etc.

Sleep.

Wake.

Mime rising, dressing, washing, eating, walking,

crapping, peeing, sitting, saying goodbye, going to work, returning etc.

While all this is going on FEMALE B now on Bed Two, gives birth. MALE A emerges from under the bed to be born through the legs of FEMALE B. They continue as before.

Male A gives baby cry.

FEMALE B cradles MALE A accompanied by lullaby music.

Couple B express joy. One pees while the other prays.

MALE A sleeps.

Couple B return to Bed Two and sleep with the child between them.

Couple B copied by MALE A growing up during the process, wake. Mime rising, dressing, washing, eating, walking, crapping, peeing, sitting, saying goodbye, going to work, returning etc. Couples quarrel. Couple B separate due to the interference of their child, MALE A, remaining on the edges of the bed.

FEMALE A is ill as all this goes on.

FEMALE A dies. Head over the end of the bed

towards the audience. She is noticed.

OTHERS

Small scream.

No music for four beats. Life goes on, the deceased is ritually but speedily shoved under the bed.

MALE A has grown up and moved to Bed One.

All back to bed.

Lie stiffly. All couples copulate.

Pee and pray.

Back to bed

Final action: birth in Bed Three, copulation in Bed Two and death in Bed One.

Freeze. Silence.

Music piece

'In bed we laugh in bed we cry' set to music appropriate to the following scene.

Foetuses

FOETUS THREE on Bed Two, curled as a foetus, hands around knees, facing the audience.

On Bed One, FOETUS ONE and FOETUS TWO, together as twins, curled around each other, sides to audience.

On Bed Three TWO BLOBS.

    Silence, heartbeat.

FOETUS ONE

    Comfortable.

    Silence

FOETUS TWO

    Warm.

    Slience.

FOETUS ONE

    Safe.

FOETUS THREE

    Listen.

FOETUS TWO

    Just listen.

FOETUS THREE

>Listen to the waters.

>*Silence.*

FOETUS ONE

>So easy.

FOETUS TWO

>So relaxing.

FOETUS ONE

>Floating.

>*Silence.*

FOETUS ONE

>I float on my sky hook.

FOETUS TWO

>I can turn somersaults.

FOETUS ONE

>I dance and twist.

FOETUS TWO

>I can do anything.

FOETUS ONE

>Life is good.

FOETUS TWO

> The colours, how they change and flit. I could look for ever. I wish I had more eyes. I see to the edge of my universe. I might be God.

FOETUS ONE

> I am learning so much. Each day my knowledge increases. Each day I find more of myself. Opportunities are endless. Each day I accomplish more.

FOETUS TWO

> All the time in tune with her, my Great Mother Earth.

FOETUS ONE

> There is so much laughing.

FOETUS TWO

> I am fed, I am fed.

FOETUS ONE

> Life is good.

FOETUS TWO

> Swinging and floating in space,

FOETUS THREE

> Connected always to the Great Mother Earth.

FOETUS ONE AND TWO

> We are free.

FOETUS TWO

> We are adventuring.

FOETUS THREE

> We are learning.
>
> *Silence. Heartbeat continues all through, very slowly, so there can be silences.*
>
> Is there life after birth?

FOETUS ONE

> Comfortable.

FOETUS TWO

> Warm.

FOETUS THREE

> What I want to know is, is there life after birth?

FOETUS ONE

> Safe.

FOETUS TWO

> Warm and comfortable.

FOETUS ONE

> Listen.

FOETUS THREE

> I am listening, and it's all very well, I agree this isn't a bad kip, in fact I don't know a better one. *Getting annoyed.*
>
> That doesn't get away from the fact that no one is answering my question.

FOETUS ONE

> But just listen and you will hear everything.

FOETUS TWO

> We are always being told things.

FOETUS ONE

> We hear it in the waters.

FOETUS TWO

> We hear it in the earth beat...

FOETUS THREE

> I have listened, I have heard and it's always the same old story, when you get as old as I am perhaps you'll understand. I'm over the hill, no longer young you might say, though I'm still developing, but now it's weight I'm gaining, nothing one can do about it. It's a question of age after all. Can't go against nature. And I'm not belly-aching about that, but at my age one just

does not accept without question all the beliefs one accepts quite naturally when one is young and impressionable. I've been in this world longer than you two. A lot longer. I've kicked around a bit. And I'm beginning to doubt. Just you think about it. All those stories they've fed us with, to be good in this life, then after birth, we'll go to our great Mother and Father. And they will love us and we'll be in their family, do you believe all that?

FOETUS ONE

Oh yes, I believe it.

FOETUS TWO

Why shouldn't it be true, why should they make up stories?

FOETUS ONE

It's so easy.

FOETUS TWO

It's so relaxing.

FOETUS ONE

I love floating.

FOETUS TWO

Rocking and swinging.

FOETUS ONE

> Why all this thinking?

FOETUS TWO

> They do all the thinking for us.

FOETUS ONE

> They do it so much better.

FOETUS THREE

> You're just avoiding the issue. You just don't want to examine the question in case there might be something in my arguments. I haven't long to go now. My time is nearly up. I've seen the signs. Heard them. I can see the birth channel opening before me. I'm not frightened of it, quite look forward to it in a way, but the question keeps nagging me.
>
> Is there life after birth?
>
> Where's the proof?

FOETUS TWO

> The fact that we're here at all is proof enough. I believe all I've been taught. I've obeyed all the rules, why shouldn't I be happy ever after?

FOETUS THREE

> Has this life always been a bed of roses?

FOETUS ONE and FOETUS TWO look at each other.

Oh no it hasn't. I heard you crying and weeping, things were not so good for you a little time ago. I heard you wail that you were in such pain you wished you could die or be born now and get it over with.

FOETUS TWO

    We all get depressed sometimes.

FOETUS ONE

    Yes, we all get depressed but that doesn't necessarily mean that one questions fundamental truths.

FOETUS THREE

    Truth? Huh. How do you know?

FOETUS ONE

    We listen and we are told.

FOETUS TWO

    We are fed by our Great Mother and we know the truth.

FOETUS THREE

    Brainwashed.

    Silence.

That's what you lot are. But tell me. Just tell me
this. Who's gone before us to come back and
tell us it's all true, that there is a great big Earth
Mummy?

FOETUS ONE

Shocked.

Don't speak like that.

FOETUS THREE

And great big Earth Daddy.

FOETUS TWO

I say cool it, man. That's enough.

FOETUS THREE

All playing happy families? All loving and
wanting you, special you, you, you, you.

FOETUS ONE

I think you should be a bit more reverent.

FOETUS TWO

About holy things.

FOETUS THREE

I think it's shit.

Crap.

FOETUS TWO

> That's too much.

FOETUS ONE

> You're going too far. Stop it.

FOETUS TWO

> There are values,

FOETUS ONE

> There are standards, that must be upheld.

FOETUS THREE

> Tell me, who's sent you a postcard saying, 'it's all true, lovely time, this is heaven they promised you?' Come on, tell me. Who's ever come back to tell? You can't say anything because no one has. There's no proof. You don't know if there is life after birth. I don't know. No one has ever come back to say it's all true.

FOETUS ONE

> I don't think you should speak about things like this.

FOETUS TWO

> It's upsetting.

FOETUS ONE

>Very upsetting.

FOETUS THREE

>Oh, I'm sorry. I get carried away. It's all... oh, why bother. But listen, I promise you something.

FOETUS ONE

>What?

FOETUS TWO

>What?

FOETUS THREE

>You know I'll be going soon. The way things are shaping up, all the growing I've been doing lately. The weight. All sure signs.

FOETUS ONE

>We've heard you say...

FOETUS TWO

>We believe you, though we've years ahead of us yet.

FOETUS THREE

>Well, I tell you, that if there is a life after birth, I'll let you know. I'll send a message, as soon as I arrive. I'll send one.

FOETUS ONE

You will? Really?

FOETUS TWO

I say, that's a wonderful idea. A good thought.

FOETUS ONE

That makes me happy again.

FOETUS TWO

Yes, very happy, thank you.

FOETUS ONE

Thank you.

Silence but continuing heartbeat.

Those other two who are in our zone don't say much.

FOETUS THREE

Oh no, they wouldn't.

FOETUS ONE

Why?

FOETUS TWO

They are far too young. Hardly started.

FOETUS THREE

Just lumps of jelly.

FOETUS ONE

>Stop that you, you're at it again. No respect for life.

FOETUS TWO

>Really, are they, just lumps?

FOETUS THREE

>Tell me, how much can you remember of your first years of life, those first three years, how much?

FOETUS ONE

>Nothing.

FOETUS TWO

>Absolutely nothing.

FOETUS THREE

>There you are.
>
>*Pause.*
>
>You were jelly too.
>
>*Laughs.*

FOETUS ONE AND TWO

>Oh, you are awful. Stop it. Shut up.
>
>*Sounds change. Heartbeats quicken. Water sounds increase. FOETUS THREE is being born.*

Birth music. FOETUS THREE is born.

FOETUS ONE

>Foetus Three, what's happening?

FOETUS TWO

>He is going. I think he's going. Listen.

FOETUS ONE

>I'm listening.

FOETUS TWO

>What can you hear?

>*FOETUS THREE is giving his birth cries, but FOETUS ONE and TWO can hear nothing.*

FOETUS ONE

>Nothing.

>*Pause.*

FOETUS TWO

>I can't hear anything either.

>*Silence.*

FOETUS ONE

>I can hear the earth beat.

FOETUS TWO

>Well, of course...

FOETUS ONE

> I can't hear Foetus Three.

FOETUS TWO

> Nor can I.
>
> *Silence.*

FOETUS ONE

> Do you think he's gone?

FOETUS TWO

> Yes.

FOETUS ONE

> I'll miss him. Even though he was rather...

FOETUS TWO

> Shush... we must listen.

FOETUS ONE

> *Whispers.*
>
> Sorry.
>
> *They both listen. FOETUS THREE cries out loud. FOETUS ONE and TWO can't hear.*
>
> We'll keep listening.

FOETUS TWO

> Just in case...

Just the sound of the heartbeat and FOETUS ONE and TWO keep listening.

Ritual bedmaking

The boxing match

This could be played on one bed only, causing the actors to be very cramped as if restricted in married life. Thus one double bed becomes the boxing ring. Alternatively, beds moved aside and one sheet placed on the floor to represent the bed/boxing ring. Ropes around the sides held at four corners by actors. Outside the ring downstage left, MOTHER OF THE BRIDE and BRIDE. Outside the ring upstage right, GROOM and BROTHER OF THE GROOM. Enter ROUND ANNOUNCER, a girl, sashaying around the boxing ring with a card on which is written: Round One 'The Meeting.'

MOTHER OF THE BRIDE

> A girl must make herself pretty. Look after her appearance. It's expected.

BRIDE

> Yes, Mammy.

MOTHER OF THE BRIDE

> A man likes a girl who looks tidy and pretty. A nice girl. Not flashy.

BRIDE

> Yes, Mammy.

MOTHER OF THE BRIDE

> He may flirt with the flashy ones, but it's the quiet girl he'll marry.

BRIDE

> Yes, Mammy.

MOTHER OF THE BRIDE

> *Tidies BRIDE's hair, brushes dandruff off her shoulders, fusses. Looks at her appearance critically.*
>
> There, that's better. Off you go dear. Have a nice time dear. I'll wait up for you.

BRIDE

> Yes, Mammy.

MOTHER OF THE BRIDE

> Maybe tonight you'll meet Mr. Right.

She giggles.

BRIDE

　Ooooooo, Mammy.

BRIDE climbs into the ring and waits in her corner, jiggling around to warm up. BROTHER OF GROOM and GROOM are drinking pints, leaning on the ropes.

BROTHER OF THE GROOM

　Shall we go down and see how's the craic?

GROOM

　Why not? In a minute, we'll go in a minute. Have another pint.

BROTHER OF GROOM

　Ah, why not?

BROTHER OF GROOM and GROOM get more pints. Drink.

　Well. We'll be off and look at the talent.

BROTHER OF GROOM

　That's the idea.

Digs brother in the ribs.

GROOM

　There was this nice little bird there last time.

BROTHER OF GROOM

> I know the one, you bastard, the red head. You might score there...
>
> *Digs him in the ribs. Laughs.*

GROOM

> Yes, she was alright...
>
> *Swill down their pints and GROOM climbs over the ropes and stands in his corner. ROUND ANNOUNCER enters and circles the ring holding card saying, Round One 'The Meeting.'*

REFEREE

> *To be improvised based on this:*
>
> Ladies and Gentlemen. Let me introduce you to the contestants in the first match of the night. In the right corner, we have Sean from Dublin...
>
> *GROOM comes forward, very macho, jiggling and gesturing to show his confidence. BROTHER OF THE GROOM acts as his second and pummels and rubs and instructs him. CROWDS cheer and boo.*
>
> And in the left corner we have the lovely Maeve.
>
> *BRIDE comes forward and jigs etc., but is much*

more feminine. MOTHER OF THE BRIDE acts as second and fusses from the corner. CROWDS cheer and boo etc.

Seconds out of the ring please.

Round one.

CROWDS cheer. Music plays 'Some Enchanted Evening' on the violin. Very.

BRIDE and GROOM advance towards each other, fists raised, and look each other in the eye. Swipe at each other, both fall to the ground, knocked out. Love at first sight. Great cheers.

REFEREE jumps into ring and pronounces a double knockout. Hauls them to their feet, they collapse over each other, then stagger to their corners where they are looked after by their seconds, BROTHER OF THE GROOM and MOTHER OF THE BRIDE. GROOM is sprawled in a chair and breathes deeply. MOTHER OF THE BRIDE sponges, pats, rubs down BRIDE.

Don't worry dear, it happens to us all, we manage. You'll be alright dear, you'll see.

BRIDE

> But Mammy... I...

MOTHER OF THE BRIDE

> Now I've done the best I could for you, given you all the help a mother can. We all go through with it...

BRIDE

> I'd like to ask you Mammy...

MOTHER OF THE BRIDE

> This is not the time for questions dear, it's time for action...

BRIDE

> Don't say things like that Mammy...

MOTHER OF THE BRIDE

> Just shut your eyes and think of the Pope dear...

BRIDE

> *Puzzled.*
>
> The Pope Mammy? I want to know...

MOTHER OF THE BRIDE

> Yes. Well, yes. Something... well... something not very nice is going to happen to you tonight. Try not to notice.

BRIDE

> Thanks Mammy.

At the other corner GROOM is being tended to by BROTHER OF THE GROOM. GROOM hawks and spits, looks impassive as he is dried and patted.

BROTHER OF THE GROOM

>Jesus. How did you let yourself in for that? My God, you got hooked this time. Jesus.

GROOM

>*Chews gum.*
>
>Uh huh…

BROTHER OF THE GROOM

>I never thought I'd see the day…

GROOM

>*Spits.*
>
>Uh huh…

BROTHER OF THE GROOM

>Still, she's a bit of alright.

GROOM

>*Leers.*
>
>Uh huh…
>
>*Sound of bell. Enter ROUND ANNOUNCER, sashaying around the boxing ring with a card*

on which is written: Round Two 'The Wedding Night.'

REFEREE

Seconds out, please.

Boxing jargon to be improvised by the actor.

Round two.

Bell. BRIDE and GROOM enter the ring and jig around, sparring and circling. GROOM advancing and BRIDE retreating. GROOM boxes with flirtatious taps. BRIDE is coy and defensive.

GROOM

How's my girl?

Jigs around and taps at her face.

Come on girl, come on, no need to feel shy, what's worrying you?

BRIDE

Retreating and keeping her hands up.

Oh Sean, it's nothing.

Moves back again.

I just am...

Do you like my nightie?

GROOM

> I do. It's lovely. You're lovely. But what about what's under the nightie?
>
> *Jigs in closer, more flirtatious jabs.*
>
> Come here girl.

BRIDE

> *Retreating again.*
>
> Oh I bought it specially. I wanted you to like it, it's so white you see... special... for... now. I want to be special for you Sean.

GROOM

> That's my girl, my pet, my beautiful girl.

BRIDE

> Oh Sean I'm glad you think I'm beautiful... I want to be... for you.
>
> *GROOM succeeds in closing in on BRIDE and knocks her to the floor. GROOM on top of her. BRIDE is aghast. REFEREE begins counting her out, pronounces GROOM the winner of the round.*

REFEREE

> End of round three.

GROOM goes to his corner. BRIDE goes to front right of boxing ring/bed.

MOTHER OF THE BRIDE

Despite the fact that in this day and age so much exposure is given to this perhaps overworked subject, sex, young women often find at the beginning of a marriage, a love affair, or a one night stand, that they...

Pause.

Don't quite, achieve the satisfaction, the pleasure, that so many irresponsible writers have led them to believe is their right. Let me tell you, it is.

BROTHER OF THE GROOM

The new virile, competent, up-to-the-minute man of this century, is sometimes a little taken aback if he finds his playmate, girlfriend, pick-up, lover, or even his wife, does not seem to share a complete experience in the love act. His technique is, of course, perfect. But it is just possible that a supremely healthy young male may inadvertently, in his eagerness and skilled approach to the art of love, overlook a minor point. Females are slow. They need arousal.

MOTHER OF THE BRIDE

Let me at once reassure anyone who finds themselves in this painful position, not to be alarmed. You are not frigid. No, you are not.

Silence.

You need to relax, get in contact with your own body.

BROTHER OF THE GROOM

Your strong body, your supple movements have already set her pulse racing, but women are demanding creatures. They need more. You must play her as if she were all the instruments of the orchestra. Give her a tinkle on the triangle, a touch on the guitar, a boom on the... drum.

MOTHER OF THE BRIDE

Stretch out your arms to yourself. Strip away those inhibitions. Learn to love yourself, before you can completely... unashamedly... open yourself to another.

BROTHER OF THE GROOM

Fingers exploring the notes on her piano, scaling and soaring the heights on the strings, deep internal resonant probes on the double bass. All your skills must be called into life, as you

open for her, new worlds, open for her new
dimensions, show her that, through you, she can
gain pleasure that she, a mere woman, could
never hope to attain... Also it should be quite a
mind-blow for yourself.

MOTHER OF THE BRIDE

Pause.

I do suggest that you attend a weekend course,
Masturbate to Love and Joy, given by Dr. Eleanor
Hotkiss. A bargain at 85 Punts. Or read Masters
Pricktease, Lovegood and Hump's exciting new
experiences, in their new book, Eat Your Way to
Better Sex, at twelve Punts and ninety five pence
plus VAT.

*ROUND ANNOUNCER circles ring with card
bearing the title: Round Four, 'The Happy
Housewife.''*

*BRIDE looks out front over the boxing-ring
ropes. She mimes an automatic movement of
washing up and putting down an object, bending
forward as if at the sink. Apron around waist.
This action is repeated continuously throughout
the following monologue.*

BRIDE

> I'm so happy.
>
> *Pause.*
>
> It's lovely to be married.
>
> *Pause.*
>
> I love being a housewife. I love doing all the things about the house.
>
> *Pause.*
>
> I'm so happy. I love getting his dinner. He loves his dinner. He loves a nice bit of juicy steak. I've been so busy. All today I've been so busy.
>
> *Pause.*
>
> I went to the supermarket and I bought meat. A nice bit of steak for his dinner. He loves steak. I'm so happy.
>
> *Pause.*
>
> We're getting everything lovely in the house. Sean bought a lovely chest the other day.
>
> *Pause.*
>
> Oh, it's lovely, just lovely, but it needs a lot doing to it. So today I French polished it. I did. I did really. I followed the instructions and I

rubbed and rubbed and polished and polished. I worked very hard.

Pause.

Then I noticed a great big crack in the floor. A big crack. All along the floor.

Pause.

So I got the Pollyfilla and I mixed it all up in a bowl and all. And I got down on my hands and knees and I filled up the crack.

Pause.

I'm so happy.

Pause.

Sean will be so pleased when he comes home and he sees I've polished his chest and I've filled up the crack. I'm so happy.

Pause.

It's lovely being a housewife.

Pause.

I'd love to have babies.

I love babies.

Pause.

We're not using... any... you know... We're not using any equipment. No, no. I wouldn't like that, I wouldn't do that.

Pause.

I wouldn't go on the pill. Oh, no.

Pause.

Our priest told me just have the first five or six, then think about Billings. I wouldn't go on the pill. No, I wouldn't like that at all. I'm just an ordinary good girl. I'm so happy. Sean will be so happy to see all I've done.

GROOM

Comes from his corner, very macho. Calls.

How's my little pet?

BRIDE

Oh Sean.

Oh Sean. I've been so busy.

GROOM

Have you, my sweet?

BRIDE

Yes, I have, you see, I polished your chest, look.

GROOM

> *Looks, but is not much interested.*
>
> Great, quite well done, pet.

BRIDE

> And I found this big crack in the floor and I filled it all up.

GROOM

> That's a good girl.

BRIDE

> I did the shopping and I bought a steak, the kind you love and I...

GROOM

> Great, is my dinner ready?

BRIDE

> Oh, Sean I'm... I... I was so very busy that I haven't cooked it yet. I won't take long, I'll...

GROOM

> You haven't? But I'm hungry!
>
> *GROOM strikes a blow and BRIDE falls down. REFEREE jumps in and counts. BRIDE rises before he finishes. Bell rings. BRIDE retires to*

her corner.

REFEREE

> End of round four.

BRIDE

> Oh, Mammy, I tried so hard.

MOTHER OF THE BRIDE

> I warned you, I warned you to always have his meal ready. There are certain things a man needs and the most important are food and drink... the other thing is, only after those.
>
> Never mind, this will all blow over.

BRIDE

> But I polished the chest...

MOTHER OF THE BRIDE

> Just don't let it happen again. I did warn you, a man expects his bit of comfort.

BRIDE

> I cleaned the house and did the shopping.

MOTHER OF THE BRIDE

> Just tell him you're sorry and you know it's all your fault, and...

BRIDE

>   Oh, I will, I will, Mammy. I'll make it all right. I will, I will.
>
>   *ROUND ANNOUNCER circles ring with card bearing the title: Round Five, 'Life's not simple."*

REFEREE

>   Round Five. Seconds out please.

GROOM

>   There's something I've got to tell you.

BRIDE

>   It's alright. It's alright.
>
>   *She pulls GROOM down towards her as she lies down to coax him to make love to her.*

GROOM

>   But I must tell you. There is something I must tell you.
>
>   *BRIDE puts her arms around him.*

BRIDE

>   Don't worry darling. It's alright. I don't mind.

GROOM

>   This has been worrying me so I must speak to you.

BRIDE

>*Pulls him to her.*
>
>It's alright Sean. I don't mind. It's alright.

GROOM

>It's hard to say these things.

BRIDE

>I know. I understand. It's alright.

GROOM

>*Bursts out.*
>
>I'm homosexual.
>
>*BRIDE swings a fist to his face and GROOM is knocked off her to the ground. Bell.*
>
>*MOTHER OF THE BRIDE becomes AGONY AUNTIE. Sits outside the ring, facing downstage, trying to compose a letter.*

AGONY AUNTIE

>Dear Worried Housewife, Your problem.
>
>*Pause.*
>
>Is one that
>
>*Pause.*
>
>I do understand.

Pause.

That difficulties like yours.

Pause. She tries again.

In the course of life one meets certain obstacles that appear insurmountable but...

She tries again.

This is a delicate subject... touching as it does... our innermost...

Pause.

The difficulties that you face are no doubt...

Pause.

Difficult, but not, of course, insurmountable. To relieve your tensions I do suggest you consult your family doctor. He will probably suggest a course of Valium.

Pause.

You should

Pause.

Get more exercise. Get out and find new interests. Stimulate yourself by trying something new.

Pause.

Exciting. As this is such a deeply personal
problem for both you and your husband.

Pause.

I feel it would be more appropriate if I were to
answer you personally, rather than on this page.

Pause.

So, if you would send me a stamped addressed
envelope, I will, of course, write to you as soon
as... Your friend, Annette Curtain.

BROTHER OF THE GROOM becomes PRIEST.

PRIEST

I'm truly glad you've come to see me, Sean.

Truly.

Pause.

Umm.

I mean that. I really do. I know it took a great
deal of personal and interior courage for you to
open your soul to me in this way. Yes, it did. Oh,
yes, it did. I can see that you're a man of deep
sensitivity. I can see that. And though I am a
professional man, believe you me I understand
the trauma it cost you. I do. Yes, truly. I mean
that. Umm. Now we mustn't be afraid of this. Oh,

no, there is nothing to be afraid of. We are in this together. I want you to feel that I'm your friend. Not to think of me as one who knows all the answers, but rather as one who... understands.

Truly. I mean that. I want you to believe that Sean. That is the key to life, Sean, understanding. Someone to trust. Knowing he's there, waiting. I mean that Sean... Truly... So Sean, am I to understand that you are saying that you are no longer sexually drawn to your wife but prefer intimacy with your own sex?

Pause.

Umm.

Pause.

Grave. Yes, grave.

Pause.

When did you first recognise the first signs of this abberation?

Pause.

Umm. I see.

Pause.

Well, of course you do realise that you are not

the first person who has approached me with problems of this nature.

Pause.

Umm.

Pause.

That incidents of this unnatural behaviour seem to be more prevalent in this day and age than in my father's time?

Pause.

Umm. I want you to realise that although I may regard your plight with personal sympathy, the Church can never condone acts that are a perversion of the natural law, which, as you know and understand, is God's Law. Even I, my dear Sean, you understand, even I cannot tamper with that. Umm?

BRIDE and GROOM now sit in the boxing ring back to back, a bit apart.

BRIDE

I can't believe it.

Pause.

That it's all happened. That he's gone.

Pause.

It doesn't seem real.

Pause.

I thought it would all be perfect. That it would be easy. I suppose things never turn out the way you hope.

Silence.

It was easier to go home to Mammy, but sometimes...

Pause.

I wish I'd stuck it out on my own.

Pause.

Mammy goes on and on. She never gives it a rest.

Silence.

I think about Sean. Can't help it. I wonder a lot. I wonder how he is, if he's alright. I'd like it if I could see him. Just sometimes.

Pause.

GROOM

It wasn't good, the way things happened. I feel guilty about it. It shouldn't have been like that. I can see that now.

Maeve, she hadn't done anything. I don't know

what to do about it. There's nothing can be done but... I'd like to see her. Talk to her, try to explain. But I don't think she'd want to see me the way things are. What can I explain? What's the point? What's the good anyway? No one can help.

Silence.

I do get lonely.

Pause.

I miss her.

Pause.

I find myself wondering,

what is she doing now?

Ritual bedmaking

Two beds to be removed as part of the ritual, carried shoulder-high by the cast. The remaining bed is then made and 'In bed we laugh in bed we cry' is sung this time to a sad variation of the theme music.

Domestic violence

One double bed centre stage. Lights up on WIFE who sits on the end of the bed smoothing the sheet of the bed she is sitting on with a repetitive movement. She is young, stout, dressed in blue. She sits with knees apart as stout women do. Her knees or her arm shakes, she tries to control this. LISTENER sits facing WIFE. LISTENER listens intently to WIFE. LISTENER shows no reaction. LISTENER is still. If possible LISTENER should not appear as man or woman.

WIFE

>*Turns to LISTENER. She speaks to but also past LISTENER. As she speaks, NURSE enters, places dressing gown over WIFE's shoulders. Exits. WIFE makes no sign of acknowledgement.*

>The doctor says it will be alright.

>*Pause.*

>That I'm not to worry about it.

>*Pause.*

>There's nothing to worry about...

>*Pause.*

>The doctor is very nice and he says I won't have

to say anything. The doctor says he'll do the talking, that they won't ask me anything... And I've nothing to worry about, he says I shouldn't worry, I should just take things easy... and ...

Pause. Silence.

I wish it was over.

Silence.

The doctor says it will be alright.

Silence.

He came home that night, just as always...

HUSBAND begins his drunken entry from upstage. He holds his right arm up, the hand limp as if it is in a sling. The actor improvises his own drunken speech.

Things were worse as the arm was hurting him.

HUSBAND curses and swears at his luck at having his arm broken and at his family. He pushes off the attentions of his wife.

I made him all comfy.

I cuddled him and tried to get him to the bed.

HUSBAND curses and swears and shoves her away. She continues to speak to LISTENER.

His arm put him in a bad temper. It happened the other week. He was raising a hammer to give me a clout.

HUSBAND raises his arm and curses her. Freezes with arm raised.

And he slipped. And the elbow broke. And it's the elbow like, it can't be put in plaster so he has it in a sling... The pains had him mad...

HUSBAND staggers to bed. He protests as he lies down. He moans and groans.

When I had him in the bed I gave him one of me nerve pills, to quieten him. I comforted him to sleep as the pains of the elbow was annoying him.

HUSBAND is nearly drifting off to sleep, still moaning.

But just as he's drifting off... The pills were working on him, up he gets out of the bed and he's all staggery with pills and the drink.

HUSBAND rises and staggers out of bed across the stage and acts as the woman describes, pulling the imaginary small children from their beds, swearing and cursing at them. Brings them downstage.

In he goes to the children and pulls them out of bed. The two of them...

HUSBAND

> *Shouts, improvises.*
>
> You little bastards... *etc.*

WIFE

> Me boy and me girl. He's seven and the little one is only four... God love her...
>
> *HUSBAND shouts and begins to grab the children.*
>
> He swings me little girl around by the hair... and he shouting and roaring.

BOY

GIRL

> *Scream.*
>
> *HUSBAND rotates as if swinging a small child by the hair with his left hand. GIRL gives piercing screams.*

BOY

> *Cries, screams, whimpers and calls*
>
> Mammy, Mammy!

HUSBAND

> *Moves in slow motion.*

You don't know what pain is. You don't know what I'm suffering with this arm.

He swings the small girl. She screams. Both BOY and GIRL sit upright, still, scream together.

I'll show you.

I'll show the both of you.

I'll show you what pain is.

BOY and GIRL scream.

You don't know the pain of it. When I'm better I'll show you. When this bollox of an arm is mended. I'll show you.

His words become slurred as if by drink and drugs.

WIFE

> *Is very firm and cold. This action has been the last straw.*

And he would.

I knew he would.

He'd broke the leg of the boy when he was two. So I knew he would.

WIFE now rises and leaves the bed and goes to HUSBAND and rescues the crying children and, as drink and drugs overcome the man, she gets him back into the bed.

I got him to the bed. And this time, the pills was working on him.

Silence.

She is now very cold, practical and detached. Deadpan.

I get the bread knife from the kitchen.

She looks expressionless toward the front as she sits by the man in the bed.

And I sticks it into his neck.

She mimes sticking the knife into the man, like an automaton. Holds still.

I stick it in lots of times, in and out.

She jabs three or four times.

The sound was awful.

A sort of crunchy sound of the knife in the flesh. On the bone. It was awful, that sound. And the blood.

WIFE leaves the man on the bed and comes to the end of the bed where she first was sitting.

Sits as before, with the same nervous twitching. HUSBAND remains still on the bed. She speaks to LISTENER.

All that blood. I couldn't bear all that blood, so I goes and phones for the doctor and the priest and the guards, and I gives twenty pound to me neighbour to look after the children and I goes off. I don't know where I been, but I went off for three days, until they found me, and brought me here.

Pause.

A real good friend paid the bail for me so I didn't have to go to...

Pause.

So I was brought here instead.

Pause.

They are quite nice here.

It's quite a nice place really. They look after you. *She laughs a little.* I have to laugh.

He only had six stitches.

Pause.

He's come up here to see me.

He brings the children. Brought me flowers.

Pause.

A real good friend paid the bail for me. Isn't that a good friend now? I'm lucky to have a good friend like that.

Pause.

My husband is a good man when he's not on the drink. He'll make the dinner. He'll come home and he'll say, 'You sit there and I'll get the dinner.' And he does. Bacon and egg and sausage and pudding and all.

Pause.

The court case. It's in a fortnight.

Pause.

I wish it was over.

Pause.

The doctor says I've nothing to worry about. The doctor says it will be alright.

They are still. Lights fade slowly. Black out.

The interval

The interval is to be part of the performance so a spot now comes up on USHERETTE with a tray of ice creams and sweets. She comes forward offering them to the audience. The rest of the cast come forward as SEX-SYMBOLS bringing the audience into the foyer for drinks, coffee etc. Inviting them as hosts. Encouraging them to see the exhibition again. They mingle for five minutes then slip away to get ten minutes rest.

Act Two

Loving couples

Three beds: Bed One downstage left, harsh white light with exaggerated shadow; Bed Two centre stage, warm soft lighting; Bed Three downstage right, half-light changing from red to green. All characters commence as children, lying spread-eagled on the floor or over beds. Silence. 'Ring-a-ring-a-roses,' is sung as they stand and become adults. They move into three couples, using the three beds, but not necessarily as beds, as sofa, a bench, etc.

They dance together to 'Ring-a-ring-a-roses' but the music changes into popular love songs (old and new).

Ring-a-ring-a-roses becomes smoochy and sexy. UPTIGHT couple, UPTIGHT MAN and UPTIGHT WOMAN on Bed One are in underwear. They are tight-lipped and disapproving and begin to dress. LOVING couple, LOVING MAN and LOVING WOMAN on Bed Two are in love and it is the first realisation of the fact. SEXY couple, SEXY MAN and SEXY WOMAN, in Bed Three, do a sexy dance and strip to the music and sing the words.

UPTIGHT couple go through a series of emotions, from

anger towards frozen silence and stiff mask-like faces, through boredom, embarrassment, irritation, bad temper, anger, disapproval, all the time putting on more clothes. They use lines of love songs, their emotions contrasting with the words. While 'Some Enchanted Evening' is heard, they show disenchantment while LOVING couple react to the same piece of music as if they were having an enchanted evening. LOVING couple move towards simplicity and openness. Meanwhile SEXY couple remove their clothes in a stripper-like manner. SEXY couple could wear grotesque masks if desired.

SEXY WOMAN

> *Sings.*
>
> Just can't get enough.

SEXY MAN

> *Sings.*
>
> Oh you beautiful doll
>
> You great big beautiful doll.
>
> *The following dialogue should be interspersed with the lines of the songs used by UPTIGHT and SEXY couples and, at times, by LOVING couple as well. LOVING couple is full of energy and joy*

LOVING WOMAN

>*Leading LOVING MAN to the bed.*
>
>We will have a vineyard.
>
>It will be warm there
>
>And we will get up early to go
>
>To the vineyard to see
>
>If the tender grapes appear.

LOVING MAN

>I will give you my loving. I raised you up under the apple tree.

LOVING WOMAN

>Pleasant fruits, new and old,
>
>I laid up for thee.

LOVING MAN

>Oh, my beloved.
>
>*They sit on the bed together.*
>
>*Love song now from SEXY couple, then in counterpoint by UPTIGHT couple.*

SEXY WOMAN

>*Sings.*
>
>Love to love you, baby.

UPTIGHT MAN

> *Spoken deadpan.*

> Younger than springtime...

SEXY MAN

> *Sings.*

> I can't give you anything but love, Baby,

UPTIGHT WOMAN

> *Spoken deadpan.*

> Can't help falling in love.

LOVING MAN

> I gave my heart to know wisdom
>
> And to know madness, folly.

LOVING WOMAN

> In wisdom is much grief.

UPTIGHT MAN

> *Spoken deadpan.*

> Love me tender...

UPTIGHT WOMAN

> *Spoken deadpan.*

> Ah, sweet mystery of life...

SEXY MAN

    Sings.

    Turn me on.

SEXY WOMAN

    Sings

    Nobody does it better.

LOVING WOMAN

    We would fence it and take the stones off the land and plant it with strong vines.

LOVING MAN

    If we made gardens and orchards and planted trees in them, of all kinds of fruits, there would be abundance.

LOVING WOMAN

    Waters cannot quench love neither can the floods drown it.

    They kiss.

SEXY MAN

    Sings.

    You must have been a beautiful baby.

SEXY WOMAN

> *Sings*

> Dirty old man...

LOVING WOMAN

> If two lie together there can be heat.

LOVING MAN

> But how can one be warm alone?

> *Looks at her. Looks out front.*

UPTIGHT WOMAN

> *Deadpan.*

> Love is a many splendoured thing.

UPTIGHT MAN

> *Deadpan.*

> When I grow too old to dream.

SEXY WOMAN

> *Sings.*

> Dirty old man.

SEXY MAN

> *Sings.*

> The look of love...

> *LOVING couple in each others arms, speaking very softly.*

LOVING WOMAN

>Come down like rain
>
>Upon the mown grass, as
>
>showers falling quietly on the earth,
>
>Come down.

LOVING MAN

>We would have midnight joys till the moon be no more.

SEXY WOMAN

>*Sings.*
>
>Something in the way he moves.

SEXY MAN

>*Sings.*
>
>That old black magic...

LOVING MAN

>Come then, my love, my lovely one, come.
>
>My dove, hiding in the clefts of the rock,
>
>In the covert of the cliff,
>
>Show me your face.

UPTIGHT MAN

>*Sings*
>
>You are the sunshine of my life.

Lines might overlap from here on.

UPTIGHT WOMAN

> *Sings.*
>
> You are my heart's delight.

LOVING MAN

> Let me hear your voice.

LOVING WOMAN

> For your voice is sweet.

LOVING MAN

> And your face is beautiful.

LOVING WOMAN

> My beloved is mine and I am his.
>
> *Others continue singing and stripping and dressing.*

UPTIGHT MAN

> La vie en rose.

SEXY WOMAN

> *Sings*
>
> I just can't get enough.

UPTIGHT WOMAN

> *Deadpan.*
>
> Loving you is easy 'cos you're beautiful.

SEXY MAN

> *Sings.*
>
> Falling in love again.

LOVING WOMAN

> Let him kiss me with the kiss of his mouth.

LOVING MAN

> For thy breasts are better than wine,
>
> Thy cheeks are beautiful as the turtle dove's,
>
> And thy neck as jewels.

LOVING WOMAN

> A bundle of myrrh is my beloved to me:
>
> He shall abide between my breasts.

LOVING MAN

> Let her kiss me with the kiss of her mouth.

SEXY WOMAN

> *Sings.*
>
> When will I see you again.

UPTIGHT WOMAN

> *Deadpan.*
>
> Some day my prince will come.

SEXY MAN

> *Sings.*
>
> I feel love.

UPTIGHT MAN

> *Deadpan.*
>
> Can't help falling in love.

LOVING MAN

> Thou art fair, o my love,
>
> Behold thou art fair: thy eyes are as those of doves.

LOVING WOMAN

> Behold thou art fair, my beloved and comely.
>
> Our bed is flourishing.

SEXY MAN

> *Sings.*
>
> Do you wanna touch me?

SEXY WOMAN

> *Sings.*
>
> Touch me in the morning.
>
> *Strippers are down to sexy underwear.*

LOVING MAN

> As the flower of the field, and the lily of the

valley,

As the lily among thorns is my love.

LOVING WOMAN

> As the apple tree among the trees of the woods,
>
> So is my beloved
>
> I stay under his shadow whom I desired and his
>
> Fruit was sweet to my palate.
>
> He brought me a cellar of wine.

LOVING MAN

> She set in order love in me.

LOVING WOMAN

> Stay me up with flowers, compass me about with apples: because I languish with love.

SEXY WOMAN

> *Sings*
>
> I can't give you anything but love, baby.
>
> *Freezes.*

SEXY MAN

> *Sings*
>
> Something in the way she moves.
>
> *Freezes.*

UPTIGHT MAN

> *Deadpan.*
>
> When I grow...
>
> *Freezes.*

UPTIGHT WOMAN

> *Deadpan*
>
> Too old...
>
> *Freezes.*

LOVING MAN

> Let her kiss me with the kiss of her mouth.

LOVING WOMAN

> For winter is past, the rain is over and gone.

LOVING MAN

> Set me like a seal on your heart.

LOVING WOMAN

> Like a seal on your arm.

LOVING MAN

> For love is as strong as death.

LOVING WOMAN

> Let him kiss me with the kiss of his mouth...

LOVING MAN

> For winter is past, the rain is over and gone.

LOVING WOMAN

>Love no flood can quench.

LOVING MAN

>No torrent drown.
>
>*Freezes.*

LOVING WOMAN

>Let him kiss me with the kiss of his mouth.
>
>*Freezes.*
>
>*Lights slowly fade, leaving uptight couple and strippers in stark silhouette,*

LOVING MAN

>Because I languish with love. Let her kiss me with the kiss of her mouth.

LOVING WOMAN

>Because I languish with love.

LOVING MAN

>Let her kiss me with the kiss of her mouth.
>
>*Lovers repeat and intertwine the words as the lights fade slowly. Perhaps soft music in the background. The words fade to whispers and finally silence.*
>
>*Blackout.*

Ritual bedmaking

ALL

> *Song during ritual bedmaking as before.*
>
> In bed we laugh, in bed we cry...

Three women alone

Note

WOMAN ONE: sensual, self-involved, unaware, blissfully happy, oblivious, satiated. WOMAN TWO: aware, hopeful, aware of possibility, nervy, in limbo, suffering, moving, alive, in purgatory. WOMAN THREE: alone, introvert, depressive, manic, masturbatory, in pain, in ecstasy, in hell, experiencing a kind of death.

The women are in three double beds in a row on the stage. Bed One is centre stage, Bed Two is stage left, Bed Three is stage right.

WOMAN ONE in Bed One, lies in the centre of the bed.
WOMAN TWO, in Bed Two, lies on the left side of the bed.

WOMAN THREE, in Bed Three, lies on the right side of the bed.

> *All lie still. Silence.*
>
> *WOMAN ONE selects a magazine from a pile on the bed to one side and reads contentedly.*
>
> *WOMAN TWO turns to left and picks up phone to the side of her bed and dials. The phone is heard ringing. There is no answer. She waits. She replaces the phone.*
>
> *WOMAN THREE slowly turns her head to the right. She lies otherwise dead still, arms stiff to her sides.*
>
> *WOMAN ONE takes a box of chocolates from beside her on the bed, takes great pleasure in selecting one. Eats with relish. Chocolate papers crackle. Reads and eats.*
>
> *WOMAN TWO tosses and turns, fidgets, gets up to look out. Returns to the phone, stares at it. Hand goes out towards the phone. Hesitates. Pulls away. Goes back to bed. Looks at the phone. Remains still.*
>
> *WOMAN THREE's arm begins to travel up the empty space beside her in the bed. She moves*

it slowly, her fingers exploring, quivering. Her body does not move.

WOMAN ONE picks up and turns on a transistor radio. It plays pop music. A love song. She munches and listens and reads contentedly.

WOMAN TWO picks up phone and dials. Ringing is heard. There is no answer. Ringing continues.

WOMAN THREE's hand and arm continue to travel up the empty bed. Her eyes move slowly.

WOMAN ONE's radio programme now becomes a joke programme.

MALE CAST

From offstage say the jokes or they could be pre-recorded and played. Continue until WOMAN ONE turns off the radio.

The bride and groom were finally alone. 'May I kiss you, darling?' he asked. 'Oh God,' she said, 'another amateur.'

Boyfriend to girlfriend, 'I dreamt about you last night.'

Girlfriend, 'Did you?'

Boyfriend, 'No, you wouldn't let me.'

Do you know? I'd only been in hospital a week when complications set in.
Why? What happened?
The day nurse caught me kissing the night nurse.

Sex. A poor man's polo.

Owner of tractor (on hire purchase) wishes to correspond with widow who owns modern Foster thresher with view to matrimony. Send photo of thresher.

I'm expecting my first baby in two months from now. We have a little kitten which I am always playing with, but friends tell me I shouldn't or my baby will be hairy. Is this true?

Doctor, how am I?
Well, I... er...
I mean, can I sit up in bed and read?
Yes, but don't start any serials.

Are you married?

No, I've always been round shouldered.

Have you heard, old Pat got married last week?

Good, I never liked the fellow.

Vicar: 'And how are you and your new wife getting on, George?'

George: 'Not so good, I'm afraid, Vicar. We've separated.'

Vicar: 'But you can't do that. You took her for better or worse.'

George: 'Yes, Vicar, but she was worse than I took her for.'

Marriage is a sort of friendship recognised by the police.

Lizzie Borden took an axe
And gave her mother forty whacks.
When she saw what she had done
She gave her father forty one.

I just bought my mother-in-law a jaguar.

Cor. I thought you didn't like her.

I know what I'm doing. It's bitten her twice already.

WOMAN ONE munches, laughs at jokes, turns pages of magazine.

WOMAN TWO replaces receiver. Ringing tone stops. Stares at phone.

WOMAN THREE lies still, her hand travelling slowly upwards.

WOMAN ONE turns off joke programme. Continues to read and eat. Silence.

WOMAN TWO, the phone rings. She jumps back in shock, picks up receiver. There is silence, a click, then dialling tone. She sits with the phone in her hand. She is still.

WOMAN THREE's hand travels as before. Closes her eyes.

WOMAN ONE crumples up a chocolate box. Puts a marker in her book or turns down the corner of a page. Washes her teeth, squats to pee, goes back to bed. Turns on transistor, jokes continue.

She snuggles down and laughs.

WOMAN TWO replaces receiver slowly.

WOMAN THREE, arm and hand continue to travel. She draws back her lips in a grimace of pleasure or pain.

WOMAN ONE puts cream on her face, looking into a hand mirror. Finds a blemish or two. The jokes continue.

WOMAN THREE opens eyes wide. Opens mouth in a grimace of ecstasy or pain.

WOMAN TWO picks up the receiver. She does not dial. Is still.

WOMAN ONE has finished her toilet. Lies down, snuggling to get comfortable. Jokes go on.

WOMAN THRE reaches her hand up and out above her head as if she is drowning, her body arched in ecstasy or agony.

WOMAN ONE puts her finger out and turns off the jokes which have now reached jokes about death.

Silence.

WOMAN TWO puts her finger on the dial. Lights begin to fade. She dials. The phone is heard ringing.

WOMAN THREE collapses, dead or asleep.

Lights out. The sound of the phone ringing continues.

'In bed we laugh, in bed we cry' song on the radio. Beds now carried shoulder-high as if coffins to the grave. Silence. Placed in new positions with the audience on two sides.

Note

This action should be developed with the actors. Is the death spiritual or physical? Does a space capture a human so that the only way out is death? Do we rely on other human beings to define ourselves? Without this definition are we already dead? What is death?

Abortion

Action on three double beds. Audience on two sides. Actors enter. HUSBAND and WIFE sit in Bed One watching an imaginary T.V., WIFE knits. GIRL sits on Bed Two. The PRIEST stands in front of Bed Three as if at an altar.

PRIEST

> *Bows in front of the altar and mumbles the prayers at the beginning of mass as in the old rite. He says the confitio as the girl speaks, speaking very low so as not to interfere with the girl's audibility.*

I confess to almighty God etc...

GIRL

> *Turns downstage*

One day I fainted.

Pause.

I knew something was wrong as I don't faint. I was working for a firm that sent me all over the place at the time.

Pause.

I just fainted.

Pause.

So I moved in with my boyfriend. He was a student then and had a bedsit.

Pause.

We didn't know what to do.

Pause.

Michael had to go to Liverpool as his Mum

lived there you see, so he had to go back in the summer. I thought I was three months pregnant.

PRIEST continues with the mass, moving behind the altar during the following conversation with HUSBAND and WIFE. Sounds from the T.V. set of a football match being played. Voices as if in GIRL's head. Voice of WIFE, HUSBAND and PRIEST. These voices would be spoken all at once, or nearly overlapping, repeated, dying and falling loudly and softly to give the impression of thoughts jumbling in her mind or imagined conversations with her parents and the PRIEST.

WIFE

> Glory be to God, how could you do this to me?

HUSBAND

> You come back here to tell us and tell us a thing like this!

WIFE

> And you expect us to be calm and take it all.
>
> That you should do such a thing to us.
>
> We gave you everything.

HUSBAND

> You had such opportunities.

WIFE

>   Now you throw them back in our faces.

HUSBAND

>   Doesn't show much gratitude.

WIFE

>   What a way to thank us.

HUSBAND

>   It must be kept quiet.

>   *All voices stop sharply. Silence.*

GIRL

>   Bless me Father...

PRIEST

>   How long is it since...?

GIRL

>   Bless me Father...

PRIEST

>   Now, my child, I will put you in touch with some nuns who will look after you until the child is born. They will find a good Catholic home for the child.

GIRL

>   I have sinned.

HUSBAND

>Through her fault.

WIFE

>Through her fault.

GIRL

>Through my most grievous fault.

WIFE

>It was no fault of your father or mine. We did everything we possibly could.

HUSBAND

>Always here to help you in any way...

WIFE

>I was always against you going to Dublin.
>
>*Silence.*

GIRL

>I walked by the river and I looked up at the trees and down at the river. I wondered why the trees did not fall on me and the river sweep me away.
>
>*Pause.*
>
>Down under me, my feet are walking. I am not connected to anything. I am not connected to myself.

Silence.

WIFE

> I don't know what I have done to deserve this.
> You come in here and brazenly tell me you're
> pregnant...

HUSBAND

> We must try and be reasonable.

WIFE

> We are your parents.

HUSBAND

> Of course we want to help.

WIFE

> But we have responsibilities to others as well as
> you.

PRIEST

> *From behind the altar.*
>
> You must be convinced that family limitation
> by artificial means is seriously wrong, and
> whatever the difficulties of the situation, you
> must be resolved now never to resort to the use of
> artificial means to limit conception.

HUSBAND

> You fail to realise the difficulties you face us with.

WIFE

> We have the rest of the family to consider.

HUSBAND

> Their morals to protect.

PRIEST

> No reason, however grave, can be put forward by which anything intrinsically against nature may become conformable to nature and morally good. Since, therefore, the conjugal act is designed primarily by nature for the begetting of children, those who, in exercising it, deliberately frustrate its natural power, and purposely sin against nature, commit a deed which is shameful and intrinsically vicious.

HUSBAND

> I have looked at this problem from every point of view. We want to help you. You know that. We are your parents, we care. But you must understand that a man in my position has to

be seen to keep up standards. This is a small community.

WIFE

In a small place like this we'd never live it down. We've always tried our best.

GIRL

Sings.

Mary had a little lamb,

Its fleece was white as snow,

And everywhere that Mary went,

The lamb was sure to show...

Silence.

HUSBAND

I trusted you, you know. You've betrayed our trust. I never believed a daughter of mine...

WIFE

No one must know. My mother must not hear of it.

HUSBAND

As she's just recovered from a stroke.

WIFE

She always had a soft spot for you.

PRIEST

>I'll remember you in my prayers, child.

WIFE

>She says the rosary for you every night.

PRIEST

>Go in peace.

GIRL

>Shit. I don't believe it. There's nothing there. They muddled the urine samples. There's nothing. Rotten little thing. There's nothing there. I'm still flat. It's all a dream and in a minute I'm going to wake and it'll all be over.

WIFE

>Jesus, Mary and Joseph, what a thing to happen in our family.
>
>*Silence.*
>
>*As she watches TV.*
>
>Ooo, look at that, Joe. Wasn't that good?

HUSBAND

>*Looking at the TV.*
>
>For Christ's sake man, will you get that ball.
>
>*Grunts.*

Kick it, can't you?

Silence as they watch.

GIRL on Bed Two, nervous. Fingers the sheet.

What did you think of him?

WIFE

What did I think of who?

HUSBAND

My God, what is he at, at all, at all? Move man, move!

You know who I mean, Mary's boyfriend, Michael.

Keeps looking at the TV.

Great. That's more like it. That's the stuff.

WIFE

Seems quite a nice young lad. I liked him. Yes, I liked him. Seems clever. Good looking too.

HUSBAND

Go on man, go on. Can't you get off your ass and move.

His family is from this part of the country though, way back. Glory be to God, did you ever see that?

Pause.

Art history!

Grunts.

What a thing to be studying. He'll make a packet out of that. Jesus, they're moving now aren't they? Come on, come on.

Pause.

WIFE

 I thought she looked tired.

HUSBAND

 That's more like it.

WIFE

 Wishy-washy.

HUSBAND

 Get in there, get in there.

WIFE

 Big rings under her eyes.

HUSBAND

 Oh, Christ. Jesus!

WIFE

 Didn't you think Mary looked pale? Joe?

HUSBAND

> Get on, you bunch of spastics.

WIFE

> Joe.

HUSBAND

> She's always looked like that. She's got a white skin.
>
> *To T.V.*
>
> Get on out of that will you!
>
> She's fine.

WIFE

> I think she looks pale.

WIFE

HUSBAND

> Oooooooooooooh!
>
> *A goal has been scored by the team they support.*
>
> *Lights down on WIFE and HUSBAND.*

GIRL

> We didn't know what to do.
>
> I thought I'd go back to Mummy and Daddy. But I couldn't. They couldn't have coped with it. I was scared. We both were scared. Nowadays I

expect it's better. I hope it's better. But then it was illegal, even in England.

PRIEST

Turns as if to preach.

Pope Pius the XII in his address to newly-weds said, 'The seriousness and sanctity of the Christian moral law does not admit unbridled satisfaction of the sexual instinct tending merely to pleasure and enjoyment. The moral law does not allow man with his reason to let himself be dominated to that point, be it a question of the substance or the circumstances of the act.'

HUSBAND

Looking at T.V.

Good man yourself.

WIFE

Looking at T.V.

Oh, he's in great form. Isn't he in great form?

GIRL

So I couldn't go home. It's a small place. If you fart everyone knows it. Dad has his job at the Tec., and Mummy, Mummy goes to daily mass even now though she's crippled with arthritis. So

I didn't tell them. There was no one I could tell.

PRIEST

Now behind the altar and is preparing to make his sermon.

Pope Pius XI said, 'No reason, however grave, can be put forward by which anything intrinsically against nature may become conformable to nature and morally good. Since, therefore, the conjugal act is destined primarily by nature for the begetting of children, those who in exercising it deliberately frustrate its natural power and purposely sin against nature, commit a deed which is shameful and intrinsically vicious.'

GIRL

Turns back to sit facing upstage as before.
Silence.

So I went to England. I just left my job and disappeared. Abandoned everything. I went to Liverpool to be near Michael. I got a temporary job. A girl on the same floor as me gave me the name of a doctor. I found him. It was in a back street. Michael helped me.

Pause.

So down I went, I didn't have an appointment, I

just went in and said, 'I hear you do abortions,' so they couldn't send me packing. He said he'd do it for forty pounds.

HUSBAND and WIFE cheer as their side wins.

HUSBAND

>They only just made it.

WIFE

>But they did, they did.

HUSBAND

>Fair play to them. It was a great match.

>*They continue to watch the celebrations with pleasure.*

GIRL

>The doctor said to lie up on the couch. He said he'd do it. He was asking forty pounds and I said I'd give him what I had. I put my legs up and he put something inside and went click, click, and he said go home and in two days it would be over.

WIFE

>*Still looking at the T.V.*

>I know what I'll do, Joe. I'll send her some vitamins. Those ones I had were a great help.

I expect she's anaemic. Most girls get anaemic from time to time.

HUSBAND

Still looking at T.V.

Well, they deserve it, they played a great game, in real good form.

WIFE

The size of the cup! Glory be to God you'd think they'd let them through though. People in crowds have no sense. Do you think the vitamins are a good idea, Joe?

HUSBAND

That feeling after a match. Nothing like it. And the first pint. My God, that's the nearest thing to heaven.

WIFE

Joe!

GIRL

I went back to my bedsit. Michael kept coming round, he was living with his Mum you see. I kept thinking...

Pause.

I kept thinking it's not working. What happens if it doesn't work?

Pause.

It's hard to stop thinking when you're on your own.

Silence.

WIFE turns off TV. They settle down for the night. WIFE says prayers from the rosary as she tells her beads, moving along a bead at a time, for each prayer. She murmurs prayers almost inaudibly. HUSBAND lies thinking, his eyes open

PRIEST

Christian married couples, then, docile to the voice of Mother, must remember that their Christian vocation, which began at baptism, is further specified and reinforced by the sacrament of matrimony. By it, husband and wife are strengthened and as it were consecrated for the faithful accomplishment of their proper duties, for the carrying out of their proper vocation even to perfection, and the Christian witness which is proper to them before the whole world.

Silence. HUSBAND turns over and goes to sleep. The Priest continues the mass. WIFE has fallen to sleep.

GIRL

> Then, on the second night, it started. Nobody was around.
>
> I didn't think it would be much then. I thought it would only be a little thing really, like a period only a bit more of it.
>
> *Pause.*
>
> The phone was downstairs so I couldn't get to it.
>
> *Pause.*
>
> I went to the toilet.
>
> *She climbs over and sits on the front of the bed.*
>
> I squatted down.
>
> *She squats down on the floor.*
>
> You know, like the native women do. Funny thing, later, when I had my little girl, they wouldn't let me squat down. It think it's the natural way but I didn't know anything then.
>
> *She bears down as if pushing out a child.*
>
> Out came a perfectly formed baby.

*She holds, as it were, a small baby that has come
from between her legs. As the baby is aborted,
the PRIEST has got to the consecration and is
raising the host. She holds the child. PRIEST
holds the host aloft. The parents sleep. All still.
Silence.*

Well not quite perfect, it wasn't ready to be born
yet. Not finished. Something was missing, wasn't
right, I don't know, but it had long little legs. I
just struggled and got a towel and somehow I got
down to the phone and rang my girlfriend, the
one who had found the doctor for me.

*She acts as if to wrap a towel around the dead
baby and sits up on the bed. Looks front.*

She got the ambulance.

PRIEST

That teaching, often set forth by the Magisterium,
is founded upon the inseparable connection,
willed by God and unable to be broken by man
on his own initiative, between the two meanings
of the conjugal act, while most closely uniting
husband and wife, capacitates them for the
generation of new lives, according to laws
inscribed in the very being of man and woman.

Silence.

GIRL

> The ambulance came four hours later. They carried me off. Michael didn't know anything about it yet.
>
> *Silence.*
>
> It was a five month baby. Five. The doctor who did it must have known I was five months gone, but was afraid I'd report him.
>
> *Silence.*
>
> It was a boy.
>
> *She weeps. She is contained. Nothing exaggerated. Recovers. Goes on. HUSBAND wakes, continues lying with eyes open.*
>
> Anyway they took me to hospital and they said that I'd have to go to theatre, and I'd have to take my ring off and I didn't want to take it off because it was the one Michael had given me. They kept asking me this and that and who the father was and I said that wasn't important and they said 'Did you have a miscarriage?' and I said I hadn't, because I hadn't, had I? They didn't believe me but they treated me well in hospital. And Mick visited me all the time.

Silence.

You know how it is if you have an ordinary miscarriage, you feel terrible. Well I felt terrible for days.

HUSBAND has gone to sleep. Both parents turn over in their sleep.

I got an infection in the hospital. A foreign doctor came in and said, 'Who the hell did the scrape?' You know, what they do afterwards. 'An awful job,' he said, because they left a lot of... the afterbirth in there.

Silence.

Michael could have abandoned me, couldn't he? But he didn't. I was lucky that he stood by me. And it wasn't his fault that he was not there at the time it happened. He was in and out to see me. But he was a student and living at home with Mummy.

Silence.

When I'm down, when I'm low and depressed, I remember.

Silence.

He would have been twenty last Thursday.

PRIEST

>   It is also to be feared that the man, growing used to the employment of anti-conception practices, may finally lose respect for the woman, and no longer caring for her physical and psychological equilibrium, may come to the point of considering her a mere instrument of selfish enjoyment, and no longer as his respected and beloved companion.

GIRL

>   I'd never do it again, myself. Never. But I wouldn't want to prevent anyone else doing it.
>
>   It would be better if they didn't have to. And this place is supposed to be Christian. What a laugh. They don't welcome bastards in this country.

Ritual bedmaking

ALL

>   *Song during ritual bedmaking.*
>   In bed we laugh, in bed we cry...

The Sacred Heart

One bed centre stage. THE SACRED HEART, the representation of the figure of Christ parting his chest to reveal his heart, stands on a cupboard to the right of the bed. Following typical Sacred Heart iconography, his head is bent to one side, one hand raised, the other points to his bleeding heart which is exposed through his bare chest. He remains quite still, with a vacant stare, red lips. Enter GIRL. She prepares the bed with the ritual bedmaking, she smoothes the sheets. She is particular, and pays attention to detail. As this bedmaking takes place the rest of the cast sings with the piano, 'Sweet Heart of Jesus,' slowly, sliding up to the high notes with wobbly voices as if a church congregation.

ALL

> *Sing.*
>
> Sweet heart of Jesus
>
> Font of love and mercy,
>
> To thee we come, thy blessings to implore.
>
> O touch our hearts,
>
> So cold and so ungrateful,
>
> And make them Lord, thine own for ever more.

Sweet heart of Jesus, we implore

O make us love thee,

More and more.

*GIRL has finished bedmaking and begins to
undress for bed, she undresses under a dressing-
gown to protect her modesty. She glances up
at the statue as she removes her clothes. The
statue continues to gaze into space with his fixed
glazed look. She is embarrassed by the statue
and picks up her night things and moves around
the bed behind the statue so as to continue
her undressing away from his direct stare. She
finishes her undressing still under the dressing-
gown and gets into her nightdress. She folds her
clothes neatly and returns to the bed. She kneels
at the foot of the statue and joins her hands, head
bowed, she says her prayers. Occasionally a few
words of prayer are heard out loud such as Sweet
Jesus, mercy, etc.*

*She leans forward and rests her head on the foot
of the statue. She makes the sign of the cross,
gently rubs the foot of the statue with her fingers
and goes to the bed and lies down. She inscribes
INRI on her forehead and snuggles down for*

sleep. She should be slightly raised on one or two pillows so that her face is clearly visible to the audience.

Silence.

Her eyes drift to THE SACRED HEART. THE SACRED HEART stares as before. Her eyes drift away. THE SACRED HEART moves his head and eyes slightly towards the girl. GIRL's eyes drift back to the statue. Then her eyes drift away, then back quickly. Has he moved? Away, back. THE SACRED HEART's eyes meet GIRL's. Hold this look. GIRL breaks away. She is drawn back. THE SACRED HEART puts out his hand slowly towards the GIRL. She, in turn, slowly puts out her hand to him. He begins to descend from the cupboard, slowly. All actions in slow motion. He moves to the GIRL. Their hands touch. He goes slowly down onto the bed with the girl. He begins the prayer...

THE SACRED HEART

> Hail Holy Queen
>
> *He lies down with the girl.*
>
> Mother of Mercy

He is lying with her as if to make love.

GIRL

> Hail our life

THE SACRED HEART

> Our sweetness
>
> *They mime the act of love and become more passionate as the prayer progresses.*

GIRL

> And our hope.

THE SACRED HEART

> To thee we cry

GIRL

> Poor banished children of Eve...

THE SACRED HEART

> To thee we send up...

GIRL

> Our sighs, mourning...

THE SACRED HEART

> And weeping

GIRL

> In this vale of tears

She is most passionate.

THE SACRED HEART

>Turn then.

GIRL

>O most gracious advocate

THE SACRED HEART

>Thine eyes of mercy towards us

GIRL

>And after this our exile, show to us

THE SACRED HEART

>The blessed fruit of thy womb.

GIRL

>O clement.

THE SACRED HEART

>O loving, O sweet virgin, Mary... Pray for us

GIRL

>O Holy Mother of God...

They are still. THE SACRED HEART sits back and brings the girl up towards him, holding her hand. THE SACRED HEART and the GIRL maintain eye contact and move always in slow motion. She sits in his arms, her head on his breast, while the rest of the cast sing 'Soul of my Saviour.'

CAST

Soul of my saviour sanctify my breast,
Body of Christ be, thou my saving guest,
Deep in thy wounds, Lord, hide and shelter me,
So shall I never, never part from thee.

THE SACRED HEART now returns to the cupboard and stands as before. GIRL lies back in bed. She makes the sign of the cross on her forehead, her lips and her breast, smiles with contentment and sleeps. THE SACRED HEART stares glassily into space. Lights fade. Blackout.

The three rooms of death

Three beds: empty bed upstage centre, in full spotlight; bed downstage right, half-light; bed downstage left in darkness gradually becoming dim light only.

OLD MAN lies in bed downstage left. He cannot be seen. OLD MAN tosses and turns on his squeaky-springed bed. He sighs and groans more or less continuously throughout.

WOMAN is in bed downstage right, half-lit. Light up on empty bed upstage centre.

WOMAN

>Mother of God, I can't stand it.
>
>*Pause. OLD MAN groans and sighs and pants.*
>
>I'll have to get another room.
>
>*She listens. Silence. OLD MAN groans.*
>
>I can't stand it. I can't stand it any longer.
>
>*Pause.*
>
>Why should I, for God's sake? It shouldn't be allowed.
>
>*Silence. Then OLD MAN groans, heaves himself in the bed.*
>
>Blessed mother have they no modesty. No shame?
>
>*Pause.*
>
>Pagans.
>
>That's what they are, just pagans.
>
>*Sighing and panting is heard from OLD MAN.*
>
>Holy Mother of God, won't they ever stop!
>
>*Pause.*
>
>They are all the same, these young ones. Once they come up to the city they behave like

animals. Filthy.

Groans and bed squeaks are heard as OLD MAN turns over and fumbles feebly for the light-switch at his bedside.

The cut of her. She so soft spoken an' all. I'd like to tell your mother what you're up to, my girl.

Oh it would turn her hair grey to hear your carryings on. You seemed nice enough when you first arrived. Respectable.

She listens. OLD MAN pants.

But just listen to you now with some lad you've got in there.

Panting from OLD MAN.

My God, I can't put up with this. Filthy animals.

OLD MAN

I need help. Oh my God, help. Can you hear me? Can you? Where is the light?

WOMAN

I will tell the landlord. He should know. He should know the unsuitable things, these goings-on in his house. He's responsible.

OLD MAN

If I had a drink... A drink would put me straight.

Bring back the strength to me.

He groans.

WOMAN

Disgusting. It's quite disgusting.

OLD MAN

Is there any light at all? Why is there no light?

He makes a feeble attempt to sit up and turn on the light. His fingers find the light-switch and a dim bedside light goes on. Only now do the audience see the old man clearly in his bed. He lies back groaning.

WOMAN

Can't you stop it?

You'd think they could leave off for one night. You'd think they could do it quietly, not like...

OLD MAN gives a load groan and pant.

Ugh. Oh, my God...

She tries to block her ears.

OLD MAN

There is no light. Where is the light?

Mother. Mammy, why did you leave me without the light?

Silence. The woman listens.

WOMAN

> *Whispering.*
>
> I hated it when I heard Mammy and Daddy. Hated it. They shouldn't have done that sort of thing. I'd put my head under the covers. I didn't want to hear.

OLD MAN

> You promised. Mammy, you promised I could have a night-light.

WOMAN

> I hated to think of them doing it.

OLD MAN

> I was good, Mother. I said my prayers. I did, I did. So why have you left me in the dark?

WOMAN

> I couldn't look at my mother in the morning. I'd keep my eyes down and she'd say, 'What's up with you? Did you have a bad dream? A penny for your thoughts.' But I'd just stare down at my plate and say nothing.
>
> *OLD MAN pants and groans.*
>
> I hated her then.

OLD MAN

>A drink. I need a drink... can hardly move the old tongue...
>
>*He groans and struggles.*
>
>Why is it dark? Where is all the light gone?
>
>*Silence for a moment, then groans and rattling breath. He struggles for breath.*

WOMAN

>They are worse than animals. Worse.

OLD MAN

>She said she'd come.
>
>*Silence.*
>
>Did she say she'd come?
>
>*He struggles for breath.*
>
>I seem to be... not too well this evening. Not too well at all.
>
>*Tries to get comfortable.*
>
>The young one. The young one said she'd look in on me. To see how I was getting on. She said she would. She might... The young one from next door.
>
>*Fumbles for the light but can't find it.*

Whispers.

Mammy, I'm afraid of the dark.

Pants.

WOMAN

> It shouldn't be allowed. I know her type, she's not married though she's got some class of a ring on her. How can she enjoy that sort of thing? She'll come to no good and I'll not be sorry.

OLD MAN

> If I could make the young one hear, she'd come. She's a nice little girl. She'd give me a bit of help. If I had a slug of whiskey now. That would do the trick, that would put me straight.

He is overcome with pain, lets out deep groans.

WOMAN

> No decent person should have to put up with this degrading filth.

OLD MAN begins to thump on the floor to get attention of the girl. He is desperate and in great pain.

OLD MAN

> Mother won't you come? And you could turn off this dark.

Continues to thump.

WOMAN

    Can't you get on with it?

OLD MAN

    Won't you come?

WOMAN

    You, you bitch, you dog and bitch in there.

OLD MAN

    Please come, Mother...

    Continues thumping.

WOMAN

    Get it over. Get on with it.

OLD MAN

    Mother, won't you come?

WOMAN

    Leave me in peace. Animals. Shitty animals, that's what you are. Beasts. Hurry and finish it. Go on, go on.

OLD MAN

    Dying.

    I'm a good boy Mother. Don't leave me. Don't

leave me without the night-light, Mother. Don't leave me in the dark...

He has a final attack and dies.

WOMAN

Hurling abuse.

You're sinners. You'll burn in hell. Stop it. Stop it. You little sods. Dirty pigs. Grunting and grovelling, you're revolting. Foul. I don't want to hear you. I'll come in and stop it if you don't... If you don't...

She is silent, listening. The OLD MAN is dead. There is silence. The WOMAN is still. She lies back on her pillows. Turns to sleep. Crosses herself automatically.

Thank God.

WOMAN settles down comfortably as if little has happened. Enter GIRL. She is singing a song. She goes to the old man's door and knocks. There is no answer. She listens, shrugs and goes to her room, the central, fully-lit bed. She sings as she throws her coat on the bed, kicks off her shoes and relaxes on the bed. Lights fade. Blackout.

Ritual bedmaking

ALL

> *Song during ritual bedmaking.*
>
> In bed we laugh, in bed we cry…

Marriage/Funeral

The beds are moved to the back and sides of the stage. Music played on the violin, changes from a celebratory jig to the Dance of Death. Begins in blackout. Lights up slowly. The cast enters one by one, dancing over the beds, until all are on the stage. Freeze. Music stops. They slowly become aware of whoever is nearest to them. They take one step towards this partner, erotically, freeze again, then move slowly to the partner, whisper. Each actor has a whisper which he or she repeats with varying emotions in his/her voice. These are whispered one by one and it may be necessary to have these pre-recorded and played on voice-over.

ALL

> *Whisper*
>
> It is most unwise for people in love to marry.[16]
>
> Men marry because they are tired, women because they are curious, both are disappointed.[17]
>
> Marriage is terrifying, but so is a cold and forlorn old age.[18]
>
> Religion has done love a great service by making it a sin.[19]
>
> Love is the history of a woman's life; it is an episode in a man's.[20]
>
> When singleness is bliss, it's folly to be wives.[21]
>
> *Woman actor.*
>
> What God hath joined together, no man shall put asunder. God will take care of that. [22]
>
> Twenty years of romance makes a man/woman look like a ruin, but twenty years of marriage makes her/him something like a public building.[23]

---

16 George Bernard Shaw.
17 Oscar Wilde, The Picture of Dorian Gray.
18 Robert Louis Stevenson, Virginibus Puerisque.
19 Anatole France, The Garden of Epicurus.
20 Anne Louise Germaine de Staël, A Treatise on the Influence of the Passions (De l'influence des passions, 1796).
21 Bill Councelman.
22 George Bernard Shaw, Getting Married.
23 Oscar Wilde, A Woman of No Importance.

The deep, deep peace of the double bed after the hurly-burly of the chaise-longue.[24] *Woman actor.*

Some of my best friends are in institutions, the institution of marriage.

Music starts up again. The actors move, in slow motion, into a waltz with their partners, eye contact but no touching. Then, as they dance, gradually, slowly touch and dance together. Music stops. Freeze.

Whisper.

It is most unwise for people in love to marry.[25]

Men marry because they are tired, women because they are curious, both are disappointed.[26]

Marriage is terrifying, but so is a cold and forlorn old age.[27]

Religion has done love a great service by making it a sin.[28]

Love is the history of a woman's life; it is an episode in a man's.[29]

---

24 Mrs Patrick Campbell.
25 George Bernard Shaw.
26 Oscar Wilde, The Picture of Dorian Gray.
27 Robert Louis Stevenson, Virginibus Puerisque.
28 Anatole France, The Garden of Epicurus.
29 Anne Louise Germaine de Staël.

When singleness is bliss, it's folly to be wives.[30] *Woman actor.*

What God hath joined together no man shall put asunder: God will take care of that.[31]

Twenty years of romance makes a man/woman look like a ruin, but twenty years of marriage makes her/him something like a public building.[32]

The deep, deep peace of the double bed after the hurly-burly of the chaise-longue.[33] *Woman actor.*

Some of my best friends are in institutions, the institution of marriage.

Waltz as before, then form an aisle either side for BRIDE to walk up. GROOM stands at the top of the aisle waiting for BRIDE, in front of him stands PRIEST. The audience should be as close as possible to the action, they should become guests at the wedding, mourners at the funeral. The actors may go forward and ask members of the audience if they are a guest of the BRIDE or the GROOM, or thank them for their flowers and mass cards. The cast hum the bridal march, 'Here comes the bride,' sounding as much as

---

30   Bill Councelman.
31   George Bernard Shaw, Getting Married.
32   Oscar Wilde, A Woman of No Importance.
33   Mrs Patrick Campbell.

possible like an organ. BRIDE totters doll-like, doing a little shuffle, down the aisle. She has a fixed, bright, doll-like smile. She smiles from side to side at the waiting guests. She stops half-way, gives a silent scream to front. Back to her totter and smile. She wears a small veil, or carries flowers. GROOM has put on a buttonhole. BRIDE arrives beside GROOM, before PRIEST. GROOM handcuffs BRIDE. They smile at each other. Silent screams to audience. Smile again. As BRIDE makes her way up the aisle again, PRIEST moves around and through the guests/ mourners and speaks to them and to the audience.

PRIEST

> The almighty Mother said: It is not good that woman should live alone. I will make her a helpmate. But among all the birds of heaven and all the wild beasts, no helpmate suitable for woman was found for her. So the Almighty Mother made the woman fall into a deep sleep. And while she slept she took one of her ribs and enclosed it in flesh. And the Almighty Mother built the rib she had taken from the woman, into a man and brought him to the woman...

BRIDE

>This is at last bone from my bones,
>
>And flesh from my flesh.
>
>This is to be called Man
>
>For this was taken from woman.
>
>*The couple join themselves together with handcuffs. Smile. Silent screams to the audience. Smile again.*

PRIEST

>This is why a woman leaves her mother and father and joins herself to her husband, and they become one body. This is the word of God the Mother. God the Mother is the head of the Church and saves the whole body, so is WIFE the head of her husband. And as the church submits to the Mother, so husbands should submit to their wives in everything.
>
>*The couple die. Hands crossed on breasts they remain stiff and are lowered back to lie stiffly side-by-side as effigies on a tomb. Cast as GUESTS/mourners stand on either side looking down at the marriage/death bed. GUESTS raise their glasses.*
>
>Wives should love their husbands just as God the

Daughter loved the church, and sacrificed herself for her church to make her holy. In the same way, wives must love their husbands as they love their own bodies. For a woman never hates her own body, but she feeds it and looks after it, and that is the way God the Daughter treats the church. For this reason a woman must leave her mother and father and be joined to her husband, and the two will become one body. She must love her body as she loves herself; and let every husband respect his wife. This is the word of God the Mother.

During this prayer, GUESTS raise their glasses and smile at the audience, throw their glasses over their shoulders. Smile very nicely. Look sadly at the audience. Look sadly at the dead couple. Sadly at the audience. Pious. Look at the couple. Silent screams to the audience. Look into the grave. Smile benignly at the end of PRIEST's prayer. GUESTS now die by kneeling down, leaning their bodies backwards, hands on chests. Music as PRIEST passes through the grave/ marriage bed.

Eternal rest give to them, Oh Mother; and let perpetual light shine upon them. Absolve, Oh

Mother, the souls of all the faithful departed from every bond of sin. And by your grace escape avenging judgement. And enjoy the happiness of everlasting life.

As the PRIEST passes over the couple, the cape around her shoulders is dropped over the couple. PRIEST turns and stands at the head of the couple.

Oh God the Mother, by your mighty power you have made all things out of nothing, and having set in order the elements of the universe and made woman to your own image. Your mercy on this your handman who is to be joined in wedlock and implores protection and strength from you. May the yoke of love and peace be upon him. Faithful and chaste, may he wed in God the Daughter; may be follow the pattern of holy women; may he be dear to his wife like Rachael.

GUEST 1

Wise like Rebecca.

GUEST 2

Long lived and faithful like Sara.

GUEST 3

> May the author of deceit work none of his evil deeds with him.

GUEST 1

> May he ever be firm in faith and in keeping the commandments.

GUEST 2

> May he be true to one wife and fly from unlawful companionship.

GUEST 3

> May he fortify his weakness by firm discipline.

GUEST 1

> May he be grave in demeanour and honoured for his modesty.

GUEST 2

> May he be well versed in heavenly lore.

GUEST 3

> May he be fruitful in offspring.

PRIEST

> Eternal rest grant to them, Oh Mother, and let perpetual light shine upon them.

BRIDE

> *Sits bolt upright from the grave/marriage bed, arms still crossed on her chest.*
>
> Do you consent to be my husband?

GROOM

> *Sits bolt upright, arms crossed on his chest.*
>
> I do, I do, I do.

PRIEST

> Now what about you?

GROOM

> Do you consent to be my wife?

BRIDE

> I do, I do, I do.
>
> *Sung as a medieval round.*
>
> To love each other truly
>
> For better or for worse,
>
> For richer, for poorer,
>
> In sickness and in health,
>
> Till death do us part.
>
> *During this song BRIDE and GROOM jump up and pose for wedding snaps. PRIEST becomes photographer.*

Poses:

1 Happy. BRIDE and GROOM, bridesmaids, Mum and Dad, jolly uncles etc., smiling.

2. Same group, drunk.

3. Farewell. The wedding party waves goodbye to BRIDE and GROOM who are leaving and turning to say farewell.

4. BRIDE and GROOM become Adam and Eve, Eve covers her breasts and genitals with her hands, her eyes raised in an expression of agony as in classical paintings. Adam covers his eyes with his hand, the other is over his genitals. PRIEST becomes the serpent, holding the apple.

5. Back to the wedding, couple become BRIDE and GROOM again, move further away, GUESTS have turned back. They are empty. Left alone.

ALL

Begin to whisper, one at first, then the rest joining in.

I do. I do. I do, I do, I do.

I do. I do. I do, I do, I do.

Until all are saying it, then breaking into song with 'To love each other truly for better or worse etc.' All sing and dance. Then all slow down as if a record is running down, as if they are puppets and are no longer having their strings pulled, BRIDE and GROOM collapse as dolls over each other. Music stops. They freeze. Silence. Then music, a waltz, all waltz to their song.

Sing.

Oh, how we danced on the night we were wed, we danced and we danced as the room had no bed.

Dance singing this song, BRIDE and GROOM lifted on the shoulders of two of the others, the waltz gets faster and faster, all spin in their couples, frantic. Sudden stop. Freeze. Silence.

Same waltz again and cast bring audience into the dancing. ALL dance.

Acknowledgements

The following songs are featured in the play:

Mary Had a Little Lamb by John Roulstone and Sarah Josepha Hale, 1830;

Sweet Heart of Jesus and *Soul of My Saviour* are hymns of unknown author and composer;

Oh How We Danced is a popular parody based on *Danube Waves* by Ion Ivanovici, 1880;

Just Can't Get Enough by Vince Clarke, 1981;

Oh You Beautiful Doll by Seymour Brown and music by Nat D. Ayer, 1911;

Love to Love you Baby by Giorgio Moroder, Bellotte and Donna Summer, 1975;

Younger Than Springtime by Rodgers and Hammerstein, 1949;

I Can't Give You Anything But Love, Baby by Jimmy McHugh and Dorothy Fields, 1927;

Can't Help Falling in Love by Hugo Peretti, Luigi Creatore and George David Weiss, 1961;

Love me Tender by Ken Darby under the pseudonym 'Vera Matson,' 1956;

Ah! Sweet Mystery of Life by Victor Herbert and Rida
Johnson Young, 1939;

Turn Me On by John D. Loudermilk, 1961;

Nobody Does It Better by Marvin Hamlisch and Carole
Bayer Sager, 1977;

You Must Have Been a Beautiful Baby by Harry Warren
and Johnny Mercer, 1938;

Dirty Old Man by George Hamilton IV, 1973;

Love Is a Many-Splendored Thing by Sammy Fain and Paul
Francis Webster, 1955;

When I Grow Too Old to Dream by Sigmund Romberg and
Oscar Hammerstein II, 1934;

The Look of Love by Burt Bacharach and Hal David, 1967;

Something in the Way She Moves by James Taylor, 1968;

That Old Black Magic by Harold Arlen and Johnny Mercer,
1942;

You Are The Sunshine of My Life by Stevie Wonder, 1972;

You Are My Heart's Delight by Franz Lehár and Harry
Graham, 1929;

La Vie en Rose by Édith Piaf, 1945;

Loving You is Easy 'Cos You're Beautiful by Minnie
Riperton and Richard Rudolph, 1975;

Falling in Love Again (Can't Help It) is the English

language name for a German song by Friedrich Hollaender, 1930;

When Will I See You Again by Kenny Gamble and Leon Huff, 1974.

Someday My Prince Will Come by Larry Morey and Frank Churchill, 1937;

I Feel Love by Donna Summer, 1977;

Do You Wanna Touch Me? by Gary Glitter and Mike Leander,1972;

Touch Me in the Morning by Michael Masser and Ron Miller 1973;

When I Grow Too Old to Dream by Sigmund Romberg and Oscar Hammerstein II, 1934.

www.ingramcontent.com/pod-product-compliance
Lightning Source LLC
Chambersburg PA
CBHW071502080526
44587CB00014B/2193